The GROSS AND GOOFY Body

It's Spit-acular!

The Secrets of Saliva

By Melissa Stewart

Illustrated by Janet Hamlin

Marshall Cavendish
Benchmark
New York

This book was made possible,
in part, by a grant from the
Society of Children's Book Writers and Illustrators.

Marshall Cavendish Benchmark
99 White Plains Road
Tarrytown, NY 10591-5502
www.marshallcavendish.us

All websites were available and accurate when this book was sent to press.

Library of Congress Cataloging-in-Publication Data
Stewart, Melissa.
It's spit-acular! : the secrets of saliva / by Melissa Stewart.
p. cm. -- (The gross and goofy body)
Includes index.
Summary: "Provides comprehensive information on the role spit plays in the
body science of humans and animals"--Provided by publisher.
ISBN 978-0-7614-4163-2
1. Saliva--Juvenile literature. I. Title.
QP191.S74 2010
612.3'13--dc22
2008033547

Photo research by Tracey Engel

Cover photo: Hammond HSN/drr.net

The photographs in this book are used by permission and through the courtesy of:
Alamy: RubberBall, 7; eStock Photo, 20; Reinhard Dirscherl, 31; FLPA, 33 (top). JUPITERIMAGES/
STOCK IMAGE, 34. *Corbis:* DLILLC, 13 (top) -Anna Peisl/zefa, 36; Matthias Kulka/zefa, 38. *Getty
Images:* ZSSD, 26. *The Granger Collection, New York:* 35 (bottom). *The Image Works:* Ellen B. Senisi,
14. *istockphoto:* Kriss Russell, 19; Paul Erickson, 41; Danny Hooks, 35 (top). *Minden:* Piotr Naskrecki,
11; Mitsuaki Iwago, 13 (bottom); Michael & Patricia Fogden, 24 (right); Stephen Dalton, 33 (bottom).
Photoedit: Davis Barber, 16. *Photo Researchers:* Oscar Burriel, 9; Cristina Pedrazzini, 24 (left); CAMR/
A. Barry Dowsett, 29; Gary Meszaros, 30. *Shutterstock:* Lukáš Hejtman, 8. *Superstock:* age fotostock, 5

Editor: Joy Bean
Publisher: Michelle Bisson
Art Director: Anahid Hamparian
Series Designer: Daniel Roode

Printed in Malaysia
1 3 5 6 4 2

CONTENTS

SPIT IT IS!

Drool. Drivel. Dribble. Slaver. Slobber. Spittle. Saliva. Sputum. Spew. Loogie. Lungie. Gob.

Who would have guessed that something as simple as spit could be described in so many ways? After all, it's just that clear, watery liquid swishing around inside your mouth.

You might think spit, or **saliva**, as doctors and scientists call it, isn't very important. But think again. You'll be amazed at all the ways spit makes life better for you and for other animals, too.

4

Know what some bats do when they're under attack? They fight back by squirting smelly spit at their **predators**. Pee-eeew!

Cats don't like to take baths, so they use their tongues and a little bit of spit to keep themselves clean.

When an archerfish is hungry, it spits at insects to knock them into the water. Then it swims over and gobbles up the **prey**.

A yellow-bellied sapsucker drills holes in trees and drinks the sugary sap. A chemical in the bird's spit prevents the trees from sealing the wounds, so the sapsucker can get all the food it needs.

WHAT IS SPIT?

Spit a little saliva into the palm of your hand. Now take a good long look. What do you see?

Spit is a clear, slippery liquid. It looks a lot like water, but it's a little slimier, and it's full of tiny bubbles. If you haven't brushed your teeth lately, your spit might also contain small bits of food. Ew! Gross! There's a good reason spit looks like water. Water is its main ingredient. But spit also contains many other things that help saliva do its job.

The slimy **mucus** in spit makes swallowing easier. **Proteins** in saliva start to break down food before it reaches your stomach. Spit also contains salts, gases, and all kinds of yucky **germs**. That's something to think about the next time someone hits you with a spitball.

Spitting in Space

If you spit in **zero gravity**, your slimy saliva will fly off into space. It might even smack someone else in the face. Luckily, researchers invented NASAdent, a foamless toothpaste that astronauts can swallow. NASAdent is also perfect for hospital patients who have to brush their teeth while lying down.

KINDS OF SPIT

Spit comes in many different forms, and each one has a different name. Here are some common examples. Can you think of more?

Drool: Stringy, slimy spit that flows out of your mouth and onto your pillow at night.

Loogie: Spit with extra mucus from the **nasal passages**. The mucus drips down the nasal passages into your mouth.

Slobber: Stringy, slimy spit, usually from a dog or other animal.

Lungie: Spit with extra mucus from your **trachea**, or windpipe, and lungs. You cough up the mucus from these areas into your mouth.

Sputum: Very thick, mucousy spit ejected from your windpipe or lungs when you are sick. It may contain some blood.

Gob: A loogie, lungie, or sputum that contains hard chunks of mucus.

What's a Wet Willy?

You're sound asleep when your annoying little brother sneaks into your bedroom. He puts his finger in his mouth and coats it with slimy spit. Then he sticks the wet finger into your ear and swishes it around. Yuck! That's a wet willy.

SPIT SUPPLY

Sublingual: These glands produce saliva with just a little bit of mucus.

Parotid: These glands produce thin, watery spit that contains chemicals to help digest food.

Submandibular: These glands make thick, slippery saliva that contains a lot of slimy mucus.

Your body is constantly cranking out a fresh supply of spit. It's produced in small sacs called **salivary glands**.

The watery mixture travels along a network of tiny tubes and empties into your mouth. You have three main types of salivary glands, and each one makes a different kind of spit.

In early summer look for masses of white, bubbly spit on tall grasses near your home. Gently wipe away the spit, and you'll find a young spittlebug. Its foamy home hides it from enemies and keeps its body warm and moist.

A spittlebug doesn't have salivary glands. To make spittle, it sucks up plant juices with its mouthparts. The juices travel through the bug's body and mix with other materials. Then white goo shoots out the insect's **abdomen**, or rear end. The spittlebug uses its back legs to whip the gooey spittle into a mass of bubbly foam.

HOW MUCH SPIT?

Like the water slowly dripping out of a leaky faucet, your never-ending trickle of spit really adds up. In just one day, most people produce enough saliva to fill between one and two 2-liter soda bottles.

Why doesn't all that liquid gush out of your mouth? Because you swallow most of the saliva you make.

Holy Cow !

Think you make a lot of spit? Consider this: In just one day, a cow can produce enough spit to fill nearly one hundred 2-liter soda bottles. Why do cows need so much saliva? Because they eat dry plants, like grass and hay. Their wet, slimy spit helps the food slide down their throats.

A Thorny Situation

A giraffe's favorite food, the acacia tree, has sharp, spiky thorns lining its branches. Luckily a giraffe make lots of thick, mucousy saliva. The spit coats the thorns and protects the insides of the animal's mouths.

GO WITH THE FLOW

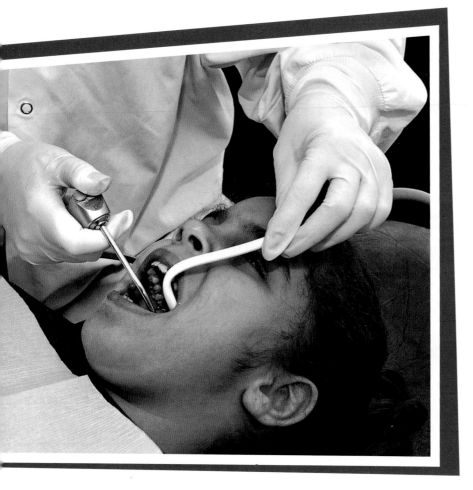

Most of the time, your mouth contains plenty of spit. But think about the last time you went to the dentist.

When a dentist cleans your teeth or fills a cavity, he or she uses an instrument that sucks up spit. It makes your mouth feel bone dry. After a few minutes, you start to get really thirsty. That's because your brain sends out messages saying you need a drink.

Ever felt thirsty, but there was no water in sight? Here are a few tricks to get your saliva flowing.

- Squeeze a few drops of lemon juice onto your tongue.

- Suck on a lollipop.

- Roll your tongue and breathe in very quickly through your mouth.

Can you think of any other ways to kick your salivary glands into overdrive?

Asleep on the Job

You make the most spit while you're eating and the least spit while you're sleeping. When you're awake, you make about 4 teaspoons (20 milliliters) of saliva an hour. During a full night's sleep (that's eight hours), you produce only about 2 teaspoons (10 ml) of spit. That's why your mouth sometimes feels dry when you wake up.

FIT TO SPIT

What do watermelon seeds, cherry pits, and brown house crickets have in common? Mix them with a little spit, and you've got the makings for some pretty amazing world records.

In 1989, Lee Wheells of Luling, Texas, set the world's record for spitting watermelon seeds. He spit a seed 68 feet, 9.25 inches (almost 21 meters). That's like spitting something over two stretch limousines placed end to end.

In 1988, Rick "Pellet Gun" Krause of Sanders, Arizona, spit a cherry pit 72 feet, 7.5 inches (about 22.1 m) at the International Cherry Pit Spitting Championship in Eau Claire, Michigan.

The current reigning champ is Krause's son, Brian. People call him "Young Gun." In 1998, Brian spit a cherry pit 72 feet, 11 inches (about 22.2 m). That's pit-posterous!

Also in 1988, Danny Capps of Madison, Wisconsin, set the grossest spitting record of all. He spit a brown house cricket 30 feet, 1.2 inches (about 9.2 m) during the Bug Bowl, an annual event held at Purdue University in West Lafayette, Indiana.

A MATTER OF TASTE

Try this. Dry off the tip of your tongue with a napkin. Then sprinkle a little bit of sugar on it.

What do you taste?

Nothing. That's right, nothing.

The taste sensors on your tongue don't work unless your food is dissolved in saliva.

Ever noticed yourself salivating, or producing extra spit, when you see or smell delicious food? Sometimes just thinking about food can prod your salivary glands into action. That's because spit plays an important role in helping you digest, or break down, food.

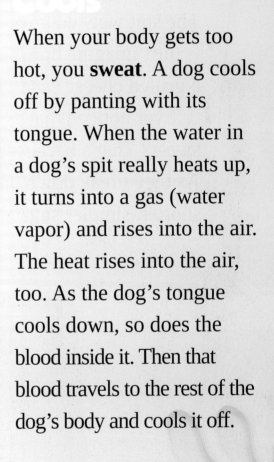

Drool that Cools

When your body gets too hot, you **sweat**. A dog cools off by panting with its tongue. When the water in a dog's spit really heats up, it turns into a gas (water vapor) and rises into the air. The heat rises into the air, too. As the dog's tongue cools down, so does the blood inside it. Then that blood travels to the rest of the dog's body and cools it off.

WET AND WILD

As you chew food, it mixes with the slippery, slimy saliva in your mouth. The spit wets your food and dissolves it so it's easier to swallow.

Just imagine how hard it would be to gulp down saltine crackers or a grilled cheese sandwich if the pieces weren't moistened with spit.

Ever noticed that as you chew a dry, salty cracker, it starts to taste sweet? That's because proteins in your spit start to digest your food. As they break down the long, complex **carbohydrates** in crackers, shorter, simpler sugars are left behind. What a yummy treat!

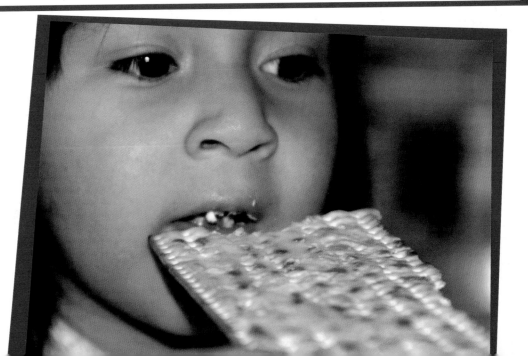

Down the Hatch

Eating a fat, round animal—like a frog or a mouse—is a bit of a trick for a long, thin snake. Luckily, the predator's slippery spit comes to the rescue. It helps the hungry hunter swallow its prey whole.

Slurp and Swallow

A housefly will eat almost anything. Luckily, its spit makes swallowing easy. At dinnertime, the insect dribbles saliva onto its food. Chemicals in the spit break down the food. Then the fly slurps it up.

RELAX AND ENJOY!

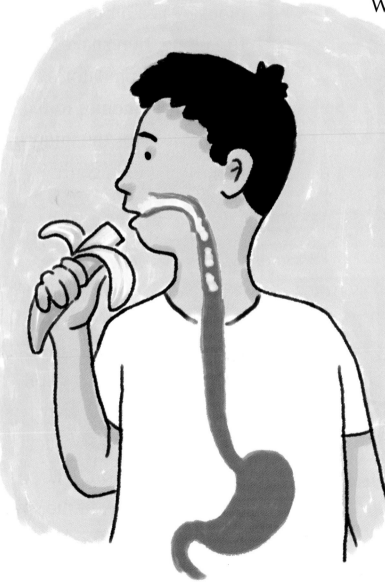

While you chew, your tongue and saliva work together. They shape your food into a **bolus**—a small round lump of mashed-up food—that slides gently down your **esophagus** to your stomach.

Think about the times you've accidentally swallowed food too soon. Remember the feeling the chunks of food caused as they scraped against the sides of your esophagus? Ouch!

If you didn't like that feeling, try chewing your food more carefully. It's better to relax and enjoy your food. The more you chew, the smoother the food's trip to your stomach will be.

Yummy in Your Tummy

Love the sweet taste of honey? Guess what you're eating? That's right—spit! To make honey, bees roll thin, runny flower **nectar** around in their mouths. As the nectar warms up, the mixture gets thicker. Chemicals in the bees' saliva break down the sugars in the nectar so the honey is easy to digest. Bee spit also helps to keep the sugary liquid fresh for a long time.

SUCK IT UP

Without spit, you'd have a tough time digesting food. But some animals would have an even bigger problem. Leeches, ticks, vampire bats, and female mosquitoes all feast on fresh blood. And they depend on proteins in their spit to keep their food flowing.

When you cut your finger, **platelets** in your blood quickly pile up and plug the wound. It takes only a few minutes for the bleeding to stop.

Platelets help you, but they're bad news for leeches and other bloodsuckers. If they didn't have clot-busting proteins in their saliva, they would starve to death.

Putting Nature to Work

Sometimes blood clogs up and **clots** form inside a person's body. If a clot blocks the blood flowing to the heart or brain, the person may die. Some scientists hope to prevent these clots with a drug made from the saliva of bloodsucking creatures. They are studying the clot-busting proteins in the saliva of leeches and vampire bats.

MORE SALIVARY SURPRISES

Surprised that a chemical in saliva can keep cuts bleeding? Then get ready for more strange and startling news about spit.

When a mouse licks its wounds, a protein in its saliva battles harmful **bacteria** that have sneaked into the cuts. Some scientists are trying to use the protein to help human cuts heal faster.

Sometimes a gila monster eats just a few large meals each year. A chemical in the lizard's saliva helps to control the amount of sugar in its blood between feasts. Scientists are using the chemical to develop a new drug for human patients with **diabetes**.

Chemicals in a pig's saliva help it attract mates. Perfume companies have tried adding these chemicals to their products, but they don't seem to have much effect on people.

Scientists have found two amazing chemicals in the spit of short-tailed shrews. One chemical could be perfect for treating throbbing migraine headaches, and it might also help reduce wrinkling. The other chemical could help lower blood pressure in patients with heart disease.

NATURE'S MOUTHWASH

As saliva swishes around inside your mouth, it scrub-a-dub-dubs everything it touches. It cleans your tongue and gums, washing away dead skin cells and the bacteria that cause bad breath. It rinses bits of food out of your teeth and leaves behind **minerals** that make your teeth strong. Proteins in spit even help prevent **tooth decay**. Every time you swallow, the bits of food and bacteria floating in spit whoosh out of sight. They reach your stomach in just seven seconds. Then digestive juices break down the food and destroy the bacteria.

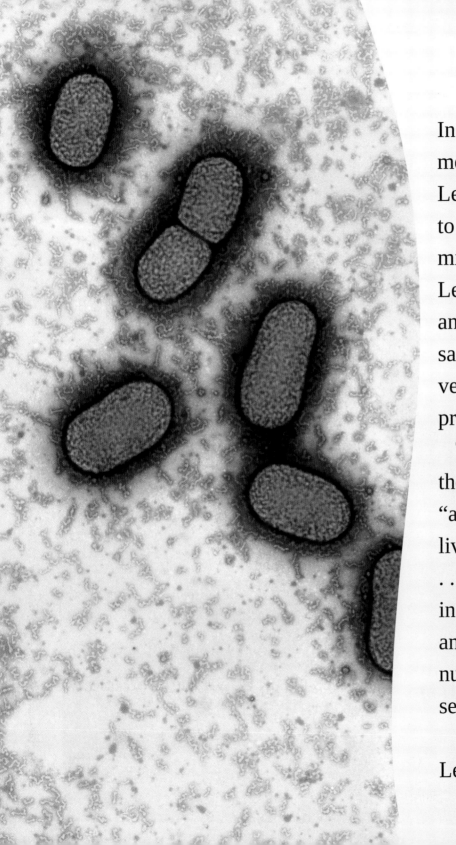

In the 1670s, a Dutch cloth
merchant named Antoni van
Leeuwenhoek was the first person
to see spit up close. Using a
microscope he made himself,
Leeuwenhoek observed saliva
and wrote down what he saw. He
said his own spit contained "many
very little, living animalcules, very
prettily a-moving."

Then he looked at saliva from
the mouth of an old man. He saw
"an unbelievably great company of
living animalcules. . . . The biggest
. . . bent their bodies into curves
in going forwards . . . the other
animalcules were in such enormous
numbers that all the water . . .
seemed to be alive."

What were the "animalcules"
Leeuwenhoek observed? Bacteria.

EAT OR BE EATEN

In the struggle for survival, some animals have come up with some weird and wacky ways to catch prey and scare off enemies.

When a short-tailed shrew bites into an earthworm or slug, its poisonous saliva **paralyzes** the prey. If the shrew is hungry, it eats the food right away. But it can also save the meal for later. The paralyzed victim won't be able to move a muscle for about two weeks.

A komodo dragon's saliva is just as deadly. It's swarming with harmful bacteria that infect wounds made by the lizard's sharp teeth. If an injured animal manages to escape, the Komodo dragon follows the animal until it dies.

Has a grasshopper ever spit on you when you picked it up? The insect's bitter spray is a mixture of saliva and partially digested food. Yuck!

Bet you can't guess how a spitting cobra uses its saliva. It's not for catching prey. It's for staying safe. When an antelope or wildebeest gets too close, the snake lifts its head and showers the larger animal's face and eyes with spit and that makes the animal feel pain. That's enough to send any creature running!

HOME, SWEET HOME

Spit can come in handy when it's time to build a home.

Know anyone with a pet gourami? When these fish are ready to mate, the male finds a clump of floating plants and builds a foamy nest in it out of air bubbles and sticky saliva. The female lays her eggs in the nest and then swims away. It's up to the male to protect the eggs until they hatch.

A female song thrush builds a cup-shaped nest in a bush or tree. She cements the materials together with wet mud and saliva. Then she lines the inside with a smooth layer of mud.

The large gray-paper nests of bald-faced hornets, yellow jackets, and paper wasps are spit-tacular, too. These insects mix chewed wood fibers and saliva to make a pulpy material. Then they build it up, layer by layer, to create the perfect home.

How does a female Eurasian swift build her nest? First, she gathers grass and feathers, roots, and bits of string. Then she uses spit to glue the materials into a rocky crevice or under the roof of a building.

SPITTING IN THE PAST

Why do most people think spitting is crude, lewd, and rude? Because spitting can make people sick. Your spit is always full of germs.

American pioneers didn't know that spit spreads diseases. They chewed tobacco all day long. And when the chew lost its flavor, they expectorated (that's a fancy word for "spit")—in the street, on the sidewalk, and even on the floor. Yuck!

Around 1840, large brass containers called **spittoons** began appearing in banks, stores, hotels, and other public places. Businesses posted signs that said,

"If you expect to rate as a gentleman, Do not expectorate on the floor."

Many towns passed laws forbidding people to spit unless their gooey gobs landed in a spittoon. That made most people happy, but who'd want the job of cleaning all those spittoons at the end of the day? Ew! Gross!

In the early 1900s, chewing gum became popular, and most people stopped chewing tobacco. Over time, spittoons disappeared and ideas about spitting in public changed.

ADAMS California Fruit Gum

Tutti Frutti Flavor

WHEN SPITTING IS FITTING

Even though people don't spit in public in most countries today, sometimes a little bit of saliva can come in handy.

• You need spit to lick envelopes and some kinds of stamps.

• Without saliva, you couldn't quickly wash a food stain off your shirt.

 • Spit even helps you play the clarinet and saxaphone.

In some cultures, people think spit brings good luck. At traditional Greek weddings guests spit on the bride's dress to wish her a happy marriage. The Masai people of Tanzania, Africa, spit on newborn babies to wish them a long, healthy life.

The Trouble with Spit

A gob of gooey spit can turn a baseball into a deadly weapon. Depending on how much slobber a pitcher uses and how he or she throws the ball, a spitball can dart wildly up, down, or diagonally. That makes it very difficult to hit. Spitballs were officially banned from baseball in 1920 after New York Yankee Carl Mays threw a pitch that hit Cleveland Indians shortstop Ray Chapman in the head and killed him.

SPIT SOLVES CRIMES

You've probably heard of **DNA**. It's the genetic material inside your cells that codes for height, eye color, and other body traits. Like fingerprints, everyone's DNA is different. That means police can use it to solve crimes.

Even when police can't find fingerprints at a crime scene, they often find traces of DNA. It's in blood and hair strands and spit.

Think of all the places where police can look for spit. It's usually on cigarette butts and empty soda cans and sealed envelopes. Even a wad of chewed gum or a half-eaten sandwich can help identify a suspect.

Police in the United States have used DNA evidence to investigate murders and other violent crimes for many years, but starting in 2006, they began analyzing DNA in less serious crimes, including car thefts and robberies. Now criminals don't stand a chance!

The Spit Kit

In 2007, bus drivers in London, England, began carrying "spit kits." When an angry passenger spits, the driver collects the saliva and turns it in to the police. Then police compare the sample with records in their DNA database. If there's a match, police track down the spitter and charge him or her with assault.

CAN SPIT SAVE LIVES?

Ever had a blood test? Bet you didn't like getting stuck with that needle. Medical workers draw blood because testing it can tell them if you're sick. But scientists now know that saliva can provide some of the same information. Soon, performing many medical tests will be as easy as spitting into a cup or licking a paper strip.

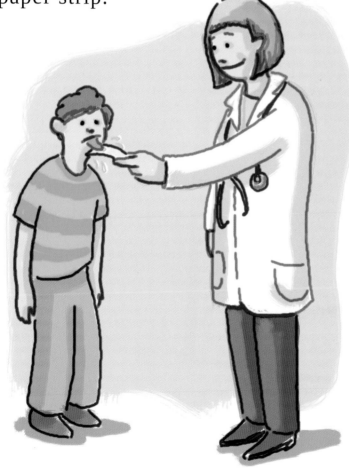

Doctors already use spit tests to detect HIV, the virus that causes AIDS, and some kinds of cancer. Tests for diabetes, Alzheimer's disease, and respiratory infections probably aren't far behind. And it may not be long before spit tests can determine your chances of developing tooth decay.

From helping with medical testing and solving crimes to digesting food and protecting teeth, it's hard to believe all the ways spit helps us every day. And we aren't alone. Many other animals depend on spit, too.

Spitting Mad

Know what camels do when they get angry at one another? That's right, they spit—in each other's faces, like this camel is doing. Llamas and alpacas do, too. Maybe they need to learn some manners.

41

GLOSSARY

abdomen—In insects and spiders, the rear body segment. In mammals, the section of the body that contains the stomach and intestines.

bacterium (pl. bacteria)—A tiny, one-celled living thing that reproduces by dividing.

bolus—A small round lump of mashed-up food.

carbohydrate—A molecule that provides the body with energy.

clot—A mass or lump. A blood clot is a mass of blood cells that can block a blood vessel.

diabetes—A disease in which people have very high levels of sugar in their blood and urine.

DNA (deoxyribonucleic acid)—A molecule with instructions that direct all the activities in a cell. It is passed from parent to child during reproduction.

esophagus—The tube that connects the mouth and the stomach.

germ—A tiny organism or particle that can make animals and other living things sick.

mineral—A molecule that helps build bones and blood cells, keeps teeth strong, and makes sure there is always enough water inside the body.

mucus—A slimy material produced mostly in the nose and esophagus. It protects delicate surfaces and makes it easier for materials to move through the body.

nasal passage—A natural air tube in the nose.

nectar—A sugary liquid that many flowers produce. It attracts insects that spread the plant's pollen.

paralyze—To make unable to move or act.

platelet—A tiny cell fragment in the blood that helps stop bleeding and closes up cuts.

predator—An animal that hunts and kills other animals for food.

prey—An animal that is hunted by a predator.

protein—A molecule that speeds up chemical reactions (such as the steps of digestion), repairs damaged cells, and builds new bones, teeth, hair, muscles, and skin.

saliva—A watery liquid that contains gases, salts, mucus, and proteins that break down food and destroy bacteria living in the mouth. It is also called spit.

salivary gland—A small sac that produces and releases saliva, or spit.

spittoon—A bowl-shaped container into which people spit chewed tobacco and saliva.

sweat—A salty liquid that is released from sweat glands in the skin. It helps humans and some other animals to cool off.

tooth decay—Damage caused by bacteria that release an acid that eats away at teeth.

trachea—The tube that connects the mouth and the lungs. Also called the windpipe.

zero gravity—A condition in which objects are weightless because the gravitational forces acting on them cancel each other out.

A NOTE ON SOURCES

Dear Readers,

Who knew spit could be so interesting? I certainly didn't until I read the article "Mouth to Mouth" by Lawrence A. Tabak and Robert Kuska in the November 2004 issue of *Natural History*. I was fascinated by the subject and wanted to know more. There was just one problem.

I couldn't find any books about spit—for adults or for children. That's when I decided to write one.

Some of the ideas in this book—especially the grossest ones—came from kids I talked to while I was doing research. Without them, I might not have thought to explain why spitballs are illegal or describe a wet willy.

Most of the information about human saliva comes from books and articles about digestion. But finding all the incredible examples of how other animals use spit was more difficult. I read all kinds of books about animals and animal behavior. I also read papers in science and medical journals, and I searched for information on the Internet.

My final step was to speak to doctors, scientists, and law-enforcement officials. These interviews ensure that the book has the most up-to-date information about the amazing ways spit is being used to diagnose diseases and solve crimes.

—Melissa Stewart

FIND OUT MORE

BOOKS

Amazing Animals of the World. New York: Scholastic Library, 2006.

Simon, Seymour. *Guts: Our Digestive System*. New York: HarperCollins, 2005.

Siy, Alexandria, and Dennis Kunkel. *Mosquito Bite*. Watertown, MA: Charlesbridge, 2006.

Stewart, Melissa. *Extreme Nature*. New York: HarperCollins, 2006.

WEBSITES

Guinness World Records
This site contains information on some of the strangest world's records you can imagine.
http://www.guinnessworldrecords.com/default.aspx

Kids Health
This site answers just about any question you might have about your body and keeping it healthy.
http://kidshealth.org/kid/

That Explains It!
All kinds of interesting information about the human body, animals, food, inventions and machines, and more can be found at this site.
http://www.coolquiz.com/trivia/explain/

INDEX

ABOUT THE AUTHOR

Melissa Stewart has written everything from board books for preschoolers to magazine articles for adults. She is the award-winning author of more than one hundred books for young readers. She serves on the board of advisors of the Society of Children's Book Writers and Illustrators and is a judge for the American Institute of Physics Children's Science Writing Award. Stewart earned a B.S. in biology from Union College and an M.A. in science journalism from New York University. She lives in Acton, Massachusetts, with her husband, Gerard. To learn more about Stewart, please visit her website: www.melissa-stewart.com.

ABOUT THE ILLUSTRATOR

Janet Hamlin has illustrated many children's books, games, newspapers and even Harry Potter stuff. She is also a court artist. The Gross and Goofy Body is one of her all-time favorite series, and she now considers herself the factoid queen of bodily functions. She lives and draws in New York, and loves it.